WHISPER

THE SONG FOR MY SOUL

KOMALIKA NEYOL

Copyright © Komalika Neyol
All Rights Reserved.

This book has been self-published with all reasonable efforts taken to make the material error-free by the author. No part of this book shall be used, reproduced in any manner whatsoever without written permission from the author, except in the case of brief quotations embodied in critical articles and reviews.

The Author of this book is solely responsible and liable for its content including but not limited to the views, representations, descriptions, statements, information, opinions and references ["Content"]. The Content of this book shall not constitute or be construed or deemed to reflect the opinion or expression of the Publisher or Editor. Neither the Publisher nor Editor endorse or approve the Content of this book or guarantee the reliability, accuracy or completeness of the Content published herein and do not make any representations or warranties of any kind, express or implied, including but not limited to the implied warranties of merchantability, fitness for a particular purpose. The Publisher and Editor shall not be liable whatsoever for any errors, omissions, whether such errors or omissions result from negligence, accident, or any other cause or claims for loss or damages of any kind, including without limitation, indirect or consequential loss or damage arising out of use, inability to use, or about the reliability, accuracy or sufficiency of the information contained in this book.

Made with ♥ on the Notion Press Platform
www.notionpress.com

For Anirudh

Contents

Preface   *vii*

   1. Why Do I Write?   1

   2. The First Ever   2

   3. I Let Love Grow On Me   3

   4. Love Knows   4

   5. I Wish I Could Be   5

   6. I Long For You   7

   7. The Birds That Remind Me Of You   8

   8. The Crescent   9

   9. To Be   10

  10. What Do I Do?   12

  11. I Am Incomplete   14

  12. Sweet Wine   15

  13. If Love Was A Person   16

  14. I Don't Know   17

  15. It Keeps Getting Harder   18

  16. The Supper   20

  17. Flowers   21

  18. In The Womb Of The Mountains   23

  19. All Paths Led To The Same Destiny   25

  20. I'll Let You Be   26

  21. Elements   27

  22. Noticed And Unnoticed   28

  23. Four Words   29

Contents

24. The Swing   30

25. It Was Necessary   32

26. I'd Still Want You   33

27. Happy 27th!   34

Preface

It was the 16th of December 2023, when I saw Anirudh for the first time. We were both at Dhamma Laddha Vipassana Meditation Centre in Ladakh, India for a 10-day silent meditation retreat. Our host was briefing the group about the schedule for the coming days when he pointed towards the high mountain that held the main meditation hall in its womb. As I turned my head to the right, this sweet man stood in his red jacket looking over his shoulder. "Good lord!", "What if he is already with someone?", and "Right now is not the time" is what I whispered to myself instantly.

One evening when I was back to my room and couldn't stop thinking about him, I heard an unknown voice in my head that whispered, "What you seek is seeking you". Somehow, that became my mantra for the remainder of the days to focus on the meditations.

On the 10th day of the retreat, we were finally allowed to talk. Anirudh and I wanted to speak to each other for different reasons, however, none of us initiated a conversation.

The next morning, we had to leave the meditation center. Anirudh's cab arrived before mine. We still hadn't exchanged a word yet. However, I had heard the sound of his laughter when he chatted with others. As he sat in the car and drove past me, all I could do was wave goodbye. In that moment, our eyes met and I saw the brightest smile I've ever seen in my entire life. The only wish I had was to keep that smile the way it was.

I thought that was the end, but the universe had different plans. It turns out that what you seek really seeks you back.

So the following morning, we both bumped into each other at the airport. We were headed back to New Delhi on the same flight.

And that's how it all began. I invited him to exchange the seat with the passenger sitting next to me. We chatted about our experiences and opened up to each other very intuitively.

We stayed in touch for some time before we finally met again.

In April 2024, we started dating but this man became the muse of my poetry ever since I saw him. However, this book only contains the chosen 27 poems since the day we confessed our feelings to celebrate Anirudh's 27th birthday.

The title of the book is inspired by Anirudh's nickname, "Roo". It is a subtle way of calling him "Rooh" which translates to Soul in Hindi. The soul breathes life into everything and holds an unimaginable amount of love. Honestly, there's no better metaphor to describe Anirudh than his own nickname.

So here begins the Whisper, the Song for my Soul, my Rooh, my Roo....

1. Why do I write?

I write so that the world will know what love means
For when all hope is gone, reminders like this breathe

I write so that when we start forgetting what newness feels like
We'll have this book to read

I write so that you live longer than me
For the songs are songs for ages, but poets die easily
I write so that you know how special you're to me
I write so that our kids know where it all started

I write, I write, I write
To preserve my sanity
I write because your love distorts the reality I lived
I write so that you can hear what you mean to me

2. The First Ever

I met her
Young as ever
Fresh as a rose
Lively as a bee
Peaceful as a butterfly
As beautiful as She

He is here
Present as being
Cheerful as a kid
Moving as time
Loving ever so lovingly
As precious as He

The home will be built
With bricks stronger than mountains
Children colourful as a kaleidoscope
Nourishment as nourishing as life
Full and empty simultaneously
The most restful, stable as certainty

3. I let love grow on me

I let love grow on me
The traces of your fingers fermenting in my bones
And the scent of your skin filling up my lungs
You, slowly intoxicating my poor heart

I let love grow on me
The softness of your embrace holding my soul
Your words penetrating deep into my consciousness
You, swiftly building your castle in my life

I let love grow on me
The twinkle of your eyes lighting up the dark hallway of my
mind
The sound of your laughter bridging the verses of time
You, gently occupying the emptiness that was

And I let love grow on me

4. Love knows

Love always softens his gaze when we meet
Holds my hand for hours, brushing his thumb on mine
Guesses songs, loves adventure, and talks food
Love looks at me admiringly while I sleep

Love can't multitask, gets annoyed, feels the fear
Still manages to crack a smile between my favourite pair of lips
Love won't let me cry, even when I say it brings peace
But love holds space for skeletons buried so deep

Love likes perfection, productivity, perseverance
But he adores my imperfections, sloth, and even fears
Love thinks I'm kind, loving, and strong
But does Love know I learn it all from him?

5. I wish I could be

I wish I could be the warm blanket
That wraps itself around you on cold nights

I wish I could be the night sky
Drawing itself like a curtain to tuck you in bed every time

I wish I could be a dream
Slowly setting you free and then all at once

I wish I could be a bird
Singing sweet melodies when you rise

I wish I could be the sunlight
Igniting your whole sky every morning

I wish I could be the wind
That touches your sweet face when you run

I wish I could be a river
Quenching your thirst after a harsh ride

I wish I could be the stalks of rice
That soften to satiate your appetite

I wish I could be all the places you go
To watch over you, to live deep inside your heart and soul

6. I long for you

We've been cursed by love
The kind where happiness doesn't last alone

Where the joy is accompanied by longing
And peace of solitude by the good times gone

Oh soul, sole you enter my heart
Stay, sober and soft, be mine

7. The birds that remind me of you

And all the birds in the sky
Remind me of you

As they spread their wings over the horizon
Kissing the sky, making love to the river

The sound of their chirps
Reminds me of your laughter

And the warm sunlight on their soft feathers
Of that sweet smile

The trails of winds they row across
Of the lines next to your twinkling eyes

And a nest for you, I build
To recover, to be loved, to fly high

The birds remind me of you
Grateful, free, and alive

8. The Crescent

It was the night of new moon
But my sky had the widest crescent in it
The one that sounds like the most precious laughter
My moon lives behind a pair of lips

9. To Be

To see your lover smile

To hear his laughter

To smell his scent on your skin

To taste the sweetness of lips

To be under the same sky

To witness his rise

To hold him when times are hard

To feel his happiness

To wipe the tears he cries

To fill his heart with love

To empty the pain he hides

To dance in the light of his twinkling eyes

To sin and wash your sins in his arms

To play with him throughout your life

To sleep with him side to side

To kiss his soft cheeks

To run your fingers through his hair

To put your head on his chest

To carry the weight of your shoulders together

To breed and be bred by the life

To fulfil the dreams

To chase the ambitions

To make it all happen

To be together
To be alive

To be, and be each other's for the rest of our lives

10. What do I do?

Tell me, oh beloved
What do I do

With these empty hands
Holding the space for you?

With my heart overflowing
With emotions my mind can't understand?

With the right side of my bed empty
For you to gently slip in?

With the wetness of my lips
Waiting to quench your thirst?

With my dreams and the dream house
Ready to turn into a reality?

With my eyes anxious
To steal another glimpse of you?

With my fears and nightmares
Where I feel scared to lose you?

With my ears desperate
To hear the sound of your laughter?

With my fingers waiting
To be locked into yours?

With all my plans wretched
By the waves from the ocean of your love?

With myself
And everything that I thought was mine?

11. I am incomplete

I always thought I was complete
A whole in itself, full and fulfilled
Until I met you

And discovered a part of me
A part that only you can evoke
A part that only you can breed
So no matter where I go now
I long for you

My happiness feels half empty
Other half, holds the space for your memories

Of beloved! When will we meet again?
When will I be fully alive again?

My heart, what is our destiny?

12. Sweet Wine

When I searched within the darkness inside me
I found the light

I found an image of you smiling
And your beautiful eyes twinkling
Hidden in the corners I couldn't reach sooner

So I got drunk on your sweetness
Only to find out you've always been by my side

You and me
we're the same child grown into two adults
we're the same souls in separate bodies, at separate times

13. If love was a person

If home was a person
You'd be the biggest castle the world has ever seen
And I'd be the princess living in it

If happiness was a person
You'd be the tears of gratitude flowing through all eyes
And the whole world would turn into an ocean

If love was a person
You'd be you and I, your hopeless lover
Lovesick, helpless, living life with my eyes closed

Love, for heaven's sake, please smile!

14. I don't know

"What is it even like to not think about you?"
"I don't know."
"Me Neither."

Oh, the awfully short conversation
Watching movie scenes over a meal
"I love you" that follows for dessert
And into each other's arms, we fall asleep

The hour of dusk visited as usual
When the angels descended from the lands of dreams
You wrapped softly in a baby pink blanket
Yawning, relaxed, and hazy

I watched it all, falling for you hopelessly
Wondering how can heavens embrace the living
How can I see magic without going blind
And yet there it was, a gentle smile

In that moment, I had everything to live for
Everything I'd ever need to breathe
All that possibly the god is made of
All that I call "You"

15. It keeps getting harder

It keeps getting harder, to tell you the truth
Every single day, you ferment deeper into my bones
So every time I have to consider the possibility
That the graveyard might scare you away
I let go of you, over and over again

I wonder to myself, if it is worth it to keep the skeletons buried
or if can I keep doing it for the rest of my life
Wouldn't it be easier to pour the poisons into your cup
And let you choose if you want a drink or not

And every time I think that you might empty the cup on my face
Burning all the cuts and wounds with sunken salt grains
I also think of your careless wide smile
When you won't have an ounce to push aside

So in those moments, I tell you the truth
I tell you how it all happened
I tell you how it all is
I tell you till I run out of words
I tell you till my heart is ready to whisper the last goodbye

I tell you till both of us are quite
And you whisper, "but I love you"

And how the three simple words
Outweigh all the pains and fears
How they make friends with all my demons
How the three simple words are heavier than my whole world

So thank you for not punishing me
For the sins that weren't even mine
Thank you for loving the truth
More than all the comfortable lies

16. The Supper

Let me feast on the sweetness of your lips
Oh beloved, set the table for the supper so warm
Pour from the saucer, into the cup of my soul
As I press my thumb against the moist forest soil

Have I ever told you, what all I've been starving for?
The soft corners of your smile
The gentleness of your breath on my neck
The gaze locked, with love and yearning adorned

The grasslands, the wetlands, and thumping pulse
The flowers, the moles, the stretch marks
The sounds of the sky, us under scorching sun
Oh beloved, keep your eyes open to light that keeps the
gardens warm

Take me to the roots that nourish the fruits
Step into the river stream with our fingers locked
A drop on my cheek, another in the womb
Oh beloved, at the shore build us a home

17. Flowers

I know you don't like the what ifs
Or the questions hypothetical
But I'd still say it

If I were a seed of lotus
You'd be the only pond I could bloom in

If I were a sunflower
I'd turn my face away from the skies and look at you forever

If I were a rose
There are no other wrists I'd rub my petals on

If I were carnations
You'd be in my every cell that gives pink

If I were a lavender
Yours is the only cup I'd ever fill with tea

If I were a cheery blossom
You're the only tree I'd ever decorate with me

If I were a jasmine

You're the only night I'd unfold myself in

If I were a marigold
You're the only garland I'd pierce myself for

But I were a wildflower
I'd grow on every inch of this planet decorating your home

18. In the womb of the mountains

In the womb of the mountains
In the roots of the trees
In the depths of the oceans
In the comfort of two arms wrapped around me

There are secrets of life, there's nourishment
There are treasures, there's freedom from my being

Thank god I can love. Thank god I can breathe.

In the wetness of the tears
In the glimpses of my favourite smile
In the light of the twinkling cinnamon eyes
In the sweetness of the cheesecake lips

There are truths, there's essence of life
There are promises, there's an eternity to live

Thank god I can cry. Thank god I can see.

In the blues of the sky
In the warmth of the glowing sun

In the whispers of the winds
In the flutter of two butterflies' wings

There are shades of future, there's a goal
There are paths to travel, there's a will to build a home

Thank god I can dream. Thank god I can hope.

19. All paths led to the same destiny

And all the paths led to the same destiny
No matter where I went, what I did
My days were filled with your memories
And nights, with the dreams of an eternity

The silence, all the sounds, and everything in between
Whispered your name, infinitely
And the things I couldn't hear
Were the depths my heart wasn't broken enough to discover

There were moments I was intoxicated with your touch
And what felt like decades, love of sobriety
Oh! How the ordinary became my extraordinary
And all the simple joys I started to seek

So I guess it all comes down to a choice
To choose you, in this and all lifetimes
How do I believe I know you not
When it feels like I've known you all my life?

20. I'll let you be

No, I wont ask you to smile
On the days you want to grieve
I won't make the stupid jokes and giggle
When crying is what you need

I won't ask you to relax
When your skies look darker than the night
No, I won't ask you to be quiet
When screaming your lungs out feels right

No, I won't ask you to stand tall
On the days you need to be in a cocoon and hide
I won't ask you to hold yourself
When letting go makes you heart open wide

No, I won't force anything on you
If that's what makes you feel light
And I'll hold space for you
At the best and the most miserable times

21. Elements

Falling like a raindrop on the clouds
Drenched in adrenaline, fear and joy
Fully alive, partly dying
My lover is a bird, singing melodies in the skies

But my lover is also a caterpillar
Hiding in the mainlands, running, climbing,
Consuming the nourishment from green life
My lover is planted in the ground

My lover breathes in the lakes and oceans,
Like a merman, he swims, jumps, dives
Bathing and drinking in his own breath
He goes deep and vast, catching corals at night

My lover loves like air, soil, and water
Yet ignites a fire every time
Soul and soulful, godly human
Oh lover, make me thine!

22. Noticed and Unnoticed

Sharp eyebrows, and hooded eyes
Cinnamon twinkles, playing with soft lines
The gaze locked, glimmers follow
Two cups of coffee, I survived

A cupid's bow, corners wide
Pigment from the roses, texture of clouds
The cheesecake lips, sweetness devoured
A smile so warm, I cried

Shy dimples, delicate moles
Soft cheeks, cheekbones like silk sheet hanging high
A kiss on the left, another on the right
Two apple halves, I bite

A thousand other little details
The noticed and unnoticed
I wonder how god made you
Perfectly imperfect, so perfectly fine

23. Four Words

Grieve, so that you can set your demons free.
Grieve, all that you need.
Grieve.
Grieve and be.

Be, so that 'You' can accept you.
Be, for as long as you need.
Be.
Be and believe.

Believe, so that you can enjoy all that springs.
Believe, for as long as you be.
Believe.
Believe and love thee.

Love, so that you can live.
Love, accept and give.
Love.
Love and just breathe.

24. The Swing

And we ran, hand in hand
Across the mountains, the grasses green
A swing awaiting, in the middle of nowhere
We ran, till we entered a dream

And we ran, till we reached the spot
Where you picked me up
My feet in the air, my heart intertwined with yours
One push, one joke, and a moment that lasted an eternity

We sat, we swung, we hugged
Kissed on the wood and ropes
Wind in my hair, my hands in yours
And time stopped, time stopped

We were kids, present, and old
A glimpse of all universes
A lifetime we lived
A world of, a world for both

And when I opened my eyes
Locked them into your own
The dream still lasted, lasted long

And I knew, I was reborn

25. It was necessary

It takes the entire world to rebuild it
Trust, heart, and faith in humanity
Yet as you heal, you realise
It was a privilege to go through all the places you've been

The lowest of the rock bottoms
Dirtiest of the nasties
Cracked bones, torn muscles, and bruised skin
All the missing pieces that should've been

Because every time a stranger smiles at you
You feel it more deeply
You learn how being cheerful is public service
Spreading it like wildfire with no murky water to extinguish it

So hold your pain close
It is also the source of strength in thee
Love, be kind, and live
All that is "you" makes an equal half of the "we"

26. I'd still want you

And even if I become everything you are
I'd still want you a thousand times
They say not to love your lover more than you
But damn, is there a single day for you I wouldn't die or live?

And even if I intoxicated my heart with all your love
My body will starve for your touch, my soul for yours
They say don't fall so deep that you can't inhale air anymore
But how do I tell them, now in the waters I breathe?

And even if I gave you all of me
Everything I'm not will long to be yours
They say love makes you insane
But how do I tell them, I don't like my sanity?

And even if I put all the starts in galaxy in a jar
It still won't glow as bright as that smile of yours
They say looking at the sun blinds you
But how do I tell them about the visions I see?

27. Happy 27th!

Everything you've ever been through
And all you are now
Is making you the person you've always dreamt to be

Accept the love this world has to offer
Let it humble you
And set you free

You live only once
Better make it worth it

Happy 27th, baby!

"No matter where the river originates from, it'll always meet the sea."

www.ingramcontent.com/pod-product-compliance
Lightning Source LLC
Chambersburg PA
CBHW031516150726
47990CB00007B/3051